W9-CAT-104

new seasons®

New Seasons is a registered trademark of Publications International, Ltd.

Written by Katie Burjek

Photography from: Shutterstock.com

© 2019 New Seasons®
All rights reserved.
This publication may not be reproduced in whole or in part by any means
whatsoever without written permission from:

Louis Weber, CEO
Publications International, Ltd.
8140 Lehigh Avenue
Morton Grove, IL 60053

www.pilbooks.com

Permission is never granted for commercial purposes.

Manufactured in Canada.

8 7 6 5 4 3 2 1

ISBN: 978-1-64030-714-8

Mother L♡VE

To the mom who gives us everything—
you deserve the world.

You can whine and complain,

but your mother knows best!

Mom, you are the smartest, strongest, sweetest person I know. I love you so much.

Our differences make us stronger.

You may be growing up and getting bigger, but I will never stop being your mom.

Moms walk in when the rest of the world walks out.

Curiosity made Mama Cat very tired.

Thanks, Mom, for everything.

On three, we pounce.

Don't mess with my mom.

Mom, what would I
do without you?

You always know how to lift me up
when I'm feeling down.

Do you see what I see?

There's nothing like the
warmth of a mother's hug.

Although we may butt heads,
I can always count on you.

There are so many things I love about you—How could I choose my favorite?

Thank you for loving me
no matter what.

Are we there yet?

Mama. Mom. Mommy.
Pay attention to me.

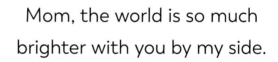

Mom, the world is so much brighter with you by my side.

You are not just my mother
—you are my best friend.

Come on. Let's play.

I hope you know that I am constantly looking out for you.

Mom, I love you
sooo much.

Kiss. Kiss.

You fill our home with
laughter and love.

A mother's love lights up the world,
even on the darkest days.

As I get older, I find myself becoming more and more like you. How delightful!

Mothers push us to reach new heights,
but are there to catch us if we fall.

I am blessed to have you as my mother.

Mom, you are caring, courageous, and wise. Never change.

You taught me to think outside the box, that anything is possible.

You make me so proud.

Thanks for helping me find joy
in the little things.

Sleep tight, little one.

Mom, you are my hero.

Come on, Mom,

my ear is really clean.

Mom, to me, you are purrfect.

My mom is the coolest cat.

Triple the fur, triple the love.

Wonderful. Wise. Watching over me.

That's my mom.

Watch me pounce, Mom.

Your constant support makes
anything feel possible.

Can I have a bite?

Mom, come on, I just want to play.

Sweet dreams.

Oh the trouble we get into together!

May our special bond
never be broken.

You have the biggest heart
and the brightest smile.
Thank you for being my mom.

Go, Team Mom!